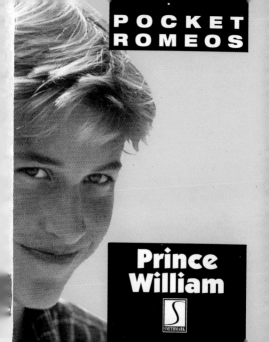

POCKET ROMEOS

Prince William

SMITHMARK

First published in 1998 by Boxtree, an imprint of Macmillan Publishers Ltd,
25 Eccleston Place, London, SW1W 9NF and Basingstoke

Associated companies throughout the world

ISBN 0-7651-0942-5

Photographs: All Action - Mark Cuthbert: 30, 36; Rod King: 25; Doug Peters: 3.
Alpha – Dave Chancellor: 5, 33, 39, 40, 44, 48, back jacket, back endpaper;
Steve Daniels: 9, 10, 13, 14, 15, 26, 47, front endpaper; S. Finn: 6. Capital –
Hugh Thompson: 22, 34, 43. Mirror Syndication International – 18. Rex – 21, 29;
James Gray: front jacket.

This edition published in 1998 by SMITHMARK Publishers,
a division of U.S. Media Holdings, Inc., 115 West 18th Street, New York, NY 10011.

SMITHMARK books are available for bulk purchase for sales promotion and
premium use. For details write or call the manager of special sales,
SMITHMARK Publishers, 115 West 18th Street, New York, NY 10011.

9 8 7 6 5 4 3 2

Designed by Blackjacks, London

Printed in Hong Kong

William Arthur
Philip Louis
Mountbatten-
Windsor was born
in London on
21 June 1982

William is 6ft 1in tall but there's still time for him to grow some more

WILLIAM LOVES SKIING

William
receives
hundreds of
Valentine cards
every year

Wills hates photographers

William once flushed Prince Charles's shoes down the toilet

William is not allowed to kiss girls in public

William enjoyed meeting Cindy Crawford and has a poster of her on his bedroom wall

Prince William's fave Spice Girl is Baby Spice, Emma Bunton

William goes to Eton College, only a five-minute walk from Windsor Castle where he sees the Queen every Sunday afternoon for tea

Wills

likes

techno

Prince William loves MTV

If he wasn't going to be king, Prince William once said he would like to be a policeman

Prince William was nearly called Arthur

Prince William is good friends with his cousin Peter Phillips, Princess Anne's son

Prince William played a lord in a Shakespeare play at school

WILLIAM HAS A DOG CALLED WIDGEON

William is especially good at painting

William regularly e-mails the Queen

On his first day at Eton College Wills signed the wrong page of the register

William prefers the countryside to the town

Wills once tried fencing but he wasn't very good at it